# HOMECOURT

i

# HOMECOURT

## The True Story of the Best Basketball Team You've Never Heard Of

by Larry Needle

Foreword by Harlem Globetrotters Legend
"Curly" Neal

New City Community Press
www.newcitycommunitypress.com

New City Community Press
7715 Crittenden St #222
Philadelphia, PA 19118
www.newcitycommunitypress.com

ISBN (PRINT): 978-0-9819560-8-4
ISBN (ELECTRONIC): 978-0-9819560-9-1

Design by Elizabeth Parks

Cover image and illustrations by Jackie Stumpf-Peters

*For Seth and Eli*

# CONTENTS

# FOREWORD

*"Curly" Neal, Harlem Globetrotters*

I was once asked how I would describe Louis "Red" Klotz in one sentence. I responded, "The little giant with the timeless two-handed set shot and game-winning smile."

Red and I were opponents for thousands of games, but this did not keep us from becoming the closest of friends off the court. We traveled the world together, playing in more than 100 countries. We entertained presidents, popes, and people of all ages and walks of life during Globetrotter games.

Some of my fondest memories with Red are exploring all the new places in which we played, looking for anything we could get our hands on to remember the trip. And, of course, I remember that night in Martin, Tennessee, in January 1971, when Red sank the game winning basket for his team...the last time one of Red's teams beat the Globetrotters. After thousands of defeats, I was happy to see Red and his guys get a win.

Red is usually perceived as being the biggest loser in sports history, but it is really quite the opposite. Before he formed the Washington Generals, he was a star player growing up in Philadelphia and at Villanova, and he later won an NBA championship. He has contributed so much to the Globetrotters and the game of basketball itself. Some of his players have gone on to play in the NBA, ABA, and some even became Harlem Globetrotters. I always thought of him as a great evaluator and developer of not only talent, but personality as well. He may have been on the losing end of the scoreboard many nights, but the laughs and thrills that we brought to audiences all over the world is what makes Red a winner every single day.

Even though our days of traveling the globe together have ended, Red still remains one of my closest friends. It is always a treat for me to see

Red, his wife Gloria, his son-in-law John Ferrari (the Generals' GM), and all of Red's children and grandchildren.

After countless games, jump shots, dunks, and pranks, the Globetrotters' show still brings joy and laughter to people all over the world.

We did it together, Red.

# GRANDPA RED

The crowd started booing louder and louder, and the Sixers' coach called for a timeout. The season hadn't been a very good one, and it was more of the same on this night. The Celtics were winning by 20, and the fans were getting restless.

"Trade 'em all!" shouted one fan.

"You're an embarassment," hollered another.

Louis and his Grandfather sat quietly, taking it all in. "These fans are pretty tough, huh Grandpa?" said Louis.

His grandfather smiled one of his big smiles. The kind Louis usually saw just before a story was coming.

"Louis, let me tell you a little bit about tough fans," he started. "Would you believe fans poking pins in your leg every time you ran down court? Or throwing bottles and trash at you? How about fans shaking the basket while you're trying to make your free throws?"

"That would never happen, Grandpa," Louis said. "That's crazy."

"I wish it were crazy, Louis. I wish it were. I think it's about time you learned about when Grandpa played basketball when he was your age, and a team from Philadelphia they called the SPHAS."

"Really," said Louis, "excited to hear one of Grandpa's stories. "Were they good?"

"I'll say," Grandpa said. "Not only were they good, they were one of the best teams in the whole world. And, Louis, would you believe the entire team was Jewish?

"How could they have been that good?" he said. "There have only been a few Jewish players in NBA history."

"This is before the NBA, Louis. This is when the game was just catching on in America in the 1920s and '30s. It was much different than the game today. Much tougher actually. The people that played were the immigrants living in the cities, and that included lots of Jewish players."

Louis knew that his grandfather, Louis "Red" Klotz, had played and coached for the Washington Generals for a really long time. They were the team that always played, and lost to, the Harlem Globetrotters. Louis loved to hear about their travels, and had been to lots of Globetrotters games himself. But he hadn't heard about the SPHAS before.

"Let's go somewhere we can talk for a while," Grandpa said. "Ice cream's on me."

Twenty minutes later, they pulled up some chairs at the ice cream shop, and Louis was all ears.

"I wanted to wait until you were old enough to hear the true story of the SPHAS," his grandfather said, "and understand what it really means. I was just about your age, 13, when I learned just how tough this sport can be," he began, "and how many lessons it can teach you...."

# CAGE MATCH

It was all Red could do to keep his cool. The other kids had been playing dirty all game, and Red had had about enough. Every drive to the basket would end in a push; every shot with a slap to the wrist or worse. These were the dirtiest players Red had ever seen.

But at "The Cage" at 5th & Bainbridge in South Philadelphia in 1933, you didn't have any refs to help you out. All you had were your teammates, your pride and your respect for the great game of basketball.

And it was a great game. Red couldn't get enough of it. Ever since he was a little kid watching his big brothers play, Red was hooked. He loved the sound of the ball being dribbled, he loved the fact that it was a one-on-one game and a team game all at the same time. And he loved that even though he wasn't one of the biggest kids, he could still be one of the best.

Now in eighth grade, Red was one of the smallest kids in his class, but he had game. His set shot was as smooth as silk, and he could handle the ball as well as anybody. But he wasn't used to it being this rough.

He had seen these kids at the Cage before, but it was his first time on the court with them. Red and his best friend Chuck had been playing pickup with a couple of other friends, when these boys challenged them to a game.

"If you're too afraid, you and your friends can just go home," one of the boys had said.

That was enough to get Red's attention. "Let's do it," he said.

"Just keep your cool out there," said Chuck.

Red loved playing at the Cage. He thought of it as his and Chuck's home court. But this time it hurt more than most. He had never been pushed into the fence so much. He knew that they were trying to bully their way to the win, but he was getting so mad that their strategy was working.

"If you want to cry to your Mommy, you can go run home," one boy said.

The other boy was yelling too, and it made Red more and more angry. He wanted to take a swing at them, but he knew that wasn't the answer. Even so, as Red got angrier his game got worse. He started throwing up longer shots and not passing to Chuck. The game ended 15-9, and Red felt as frustrated as he ever had on the court.

"Let's do it again sometime if you boys didn't get enough," one boy yelled.

"Don't worry, we'll be back sure enough," said Red, trying hard to fight back his emotions as they started towards home.

"You know we're better than they are," Red said to Chuck. "I just got so mad that I couldn't think straight."

"I know," said Chuck, "Me too. I think that was their plan." They headed up the street, past blocks of South Philly row homes, kids playing basketball on almost every corner.

"Why do you think they're so mean anyway?" Red asked.

"You know, my Dad always tells me that people who are mean like that are just really unhappy inside, and need to yell at other people to make themselves feel better," said Chuck.

'I guess," said Red, "They must be really unhappy then."

"Let's go home pal," Chuck said. "Who needs those guys anyway."

# LESSONS AT HOME

His real name was Louis, but everyone called him "Red" or "Reds" for as long as he could remember. His shiny red hair made it a pretty easy choice for a nickname. He and his buddy Chuck could hardly be separated. Although Chuck lived a few miles away in the Frankford part of town, they had met playing basketball and been playing together ever since.

When they got home, Red quickly realized he was late… again. "Chaim Lab, where have you been?" his mother called. "It's Friday night and we need to say the blessings," she said. "Everyone's ready for dinner."

Red loved when his mother called him that. Chaim Lab meant "my love" in Yiddish, and it always felt good to hear. The good feelings were short-lived, though, as his father began to yell in Russian. That was never a good sign.

Red could make out a few of the words, enough to know that it wasn't pleasant. His parents had both immigrated from Russia as children, and met and married in Philadelphia. His father was a cabinet maker, one of the best in the city.

"You and this basketball," his father said. "Why aren't you helping me in the shop like your brothers? Do you really think that someone your size will ever get anywhere playing basketball?"

"I'm not trying to get anywhere sir," Red said softly, "I just want to play with my friends."

"Well, while you're playing, the rest of us are working and trying to put some food on the table," his father said. "How much basketball can one boy play?"

His brother Sam flashed him a mean look, and they sat down for Friday night prayers and a delicious dinner. All the while though, Red couldn't help but think about the game and those boys.

"Why are some of the kids so mean to us?" Red asked. "Is it just because we're Jewish?"

"It's possible," his mother said. "There's no good reason of course, but they get it from their parents. It's all this talk of the Nazis everywhere, and the children think it's OK to act that way too."

"It doesn't make sense," Red said. "We didn't do anything to them. Next time, I'm not sure if I can keep my cool."

His father glared at him. "Why don't you make sure there's not a next time," he said. "Start helping us in the shop more and play your sport less, and you won't have these problems."

"It's not worth it Louis," his mother said. "You know one of your grandmother's favorite Yiddish expressions: 'Ten kisses do not make up for one slap'."

"Don't worry Mom, I don't plan on doing either," Red said as he kept eating.

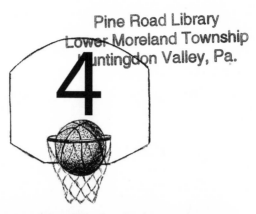

# SATURDAYS AT THE BROADWOOD

Saturday was the Sabbath, or Shabbat, and Red always enjoyed going to synagogue with his family. All of his friends were there with their families, and everyone got together afterwards for a huge lunch at the social hall. But he especially enjoyed Saturdays because of what was to come that night.

Red pulled his normal routine. After Shabbat was officially over at sundown, he'd go up to his room, pack up his basketball clothes, throw his gym bag out the bedroom window to the alley below and head downstairs.

"And where do you think you're going, young man?" his mother called sweetly from the kitchen.

"To hang out with Chuck and some friends," Red said. "Can I please?" Red felt terrible lying to his mother, but he was sure he knew what the answer would be if he asked to play."

"Be back by 10," called his Mother.

"I will," Red shouted as he zoomed out the back door. He grabbed his gym bag in the alley, and went down to the corner to meet Chuck and catch the next trolley. He changed into his basketball gear in the back of the train, and, before he knew it, he arrived at his favorite place in the whole world – the Broadwood Hotel.

It didn't get any better than Saturday night at the Broadwood, because that was home court for the SPHAS, the best basketball team Red had ever seen. The SPHAS – representing the South Philadelphia Hebrew Association—were definitely the best team in the city, and, as far as Red was concerned, probably the best in the whole world.

Red loved to watch them. There was Gil Fitch, Lou Forman, Shikey Gotthofer, Cy Kaselman, Inky Lautman, Harry Litwack and Red Wolfe.They made basketball look like a whole different game. The passing was crisp and fast, and the shooting was amazing. Most other teams had no chance.

They had won three Eastern League championships in the past four years under their head coach, Eddie Gottlieb, beating teams like the Trenton Moose, Brooklyn Visitations and the New York Celtics. They were now in the American Basketball League, and facing even tougher competition from up and down the east coast.

The scene at the Broadwood was amazing. People would come from all over town to see the SPHAS. They would get all dressed up for the games, and the dancing that followed afterwards.
The line would start forming an hour early, with everyone trying to get a good seat. It was 65 cents

for men and 35 cents for women. Hot dogs were a dime each. During the game, the PA announcer would give away a salami, and the lucky number winner always got a brand new $20 suit from Gerson's store.

Red and Chuck loved to be there for the SPHAS games, but they weren't only there to *watch* basketball. A few months earlier, they both tried out for and made the SPHAS youth team, called the Outlaws. So, before every SPHAS home game, the boys got to play in a game of their own. That was the best. They were able to play in front of a crowd, and then stay to watch the real SPHAS afterwards.

"REEEEEDDDDDDD KKKLOTTTTZZZZ," the announcer said, introducing each player as the Outlaws took the floor. It always gave Red chills to hear his name announced. Mr. Zinkoff, the PA announcer, had a special way to say everyone's name that made it really fun.

Red couldn't decide what he liked more – playing in the early game, or watching the SPHAS afterwards. On this night, he and Chuck were unstoppable. They played a team from the YMHA, and Red's outside shooting was on.

He and Chuck led the way for a 22-14 win, and the SPHAS players all shook hands with the kids as they left the court.  Red looked up at them with a twinkle in his eye.  That will be me and Chuck playing for the SPHAS one day, Red thought to himself.

# LET YOUR GAME
# DO YOUR TALKING

Even on the SPHAS' homecourt at the Broadwood, the crowd was never fully supportive. Since the team was known to have all Jewish players, the stands usually included at least a handful of anti-Semitic fans rooting against the SPHAS, and they could get pretty nasty.

But Red heard that the road trips were much worse. Sometimes, fans would throw bottles or trash at the players. Just last week, someone said that a fan in Brooklyn jammed a lit cigar into one of the player's legs. And an old lady at the Trenton games kept poking a hatpin at the players every time they ran down court. Unbelievable.

But it hardly seemed to bother the players at all. In fact, the louder the fans were yelling at them, the better they seemed to play. In previous years, they even wore jerseys with big Hebrew letters on them. Red figured that they probably wanted to make sure the other teams remembered it as an all-Jewish team they were playing... and losing to.

On this night, the Trenton Bombers had no chance. The SPHAS' teamwork was flawless. It seemed like there were at least five passes every time down court, and someone always found the open man.

Of course, that didn't stop Coach Gottlieb from yelling at the refs and his players almost the whole game. Coach Eddie Gottlieb, or "Gotty" as they called him, just couldn't sit still – waving his arms, tugging at his tie and pacing up and down the sideline. By the end of the game, he was as sweaty as the players.

The SPHAS' combination of quickness, ball-handling and teamwork was more than the Bombers could handle, and it was an easy 54-38 win.

After the game, Gil Fitch, one of the team's best players, was the first one off the court to head for the shower. And with good reason. He would put on a suit and came back a few minutes later to serve as bandleader for the big dance. Everyone emptied from the stands onto the court, which now was a huge dance floor. Red and Chuck watched in amazement.

"What'd you think of the game, kid?" someone said to Red. He turned to see that it was Cy Kaselman, his favorite player, now dressed in a suit and tie.

"It was amazing, Mr. Kaselman," Red stuttered. "You couldn't miss, and you must have had 10 steals."

"Remember, it's all about the defense, you two," he said. "Anyone can hit a set shot, but defense is where you win the games."

"I know, but how do you put up with all of that badgering from the fans?" Red asked. "I woulda jumped in the second row and punched out that one guy."

"You know Red," he said, "I used to feel that way too, but Coach Gottlieb convinced us that we can do our best talking with our basketball. There's no better way to make those guys quiet than to beat them fair and square and leave them speechless."

"I guess you're right," said Red.

"I think we actually help to change how people see us, which is the best part," Kaselman said. "They soon realize that Jewish people can do everything that anyone else can do. That people are really all the same no matter their religion or color or anything else."

"I guess so," said Red. "Seems like most of them could use a little lesson anyway."

"Don't let it get you down kid," he said. "Just keep shooting, and let your game do your talking. You'll see how good that can feel."

Red knew that he was right. When they saw that it was almost 9:30, they said a quick goodbye and started running for the next trolley home.

# COACH GOTTY

Most days after school, Red and Chuck would go to the Outlaws practice, and stick around to see the SPHAS work out.   Some days they'd even get to help out as ballboys, and be a part of the team's drills.

During a break, Coach Gottlieb called over to them. "Hey kids," he hollered, "get over here."  They sprinted over, hoping they weren't in trouble for something.

"You guys have been practicing hard, and helping out around here. I appreciate that. You two think you want to play for the SPHAS one day?" he asked.

"More than anything Coach," Red blurted out. "It's the best basketball team in the world."

"Only on some nights kid," said Coach, "but we're trying. You need to have pretty thick skin to be on this team though. Do you guys think you can take the heat?"

"I think so Coach," said Chuck, "when we're a little older anyway. We hear that the road trips are crazy though."

"You can say that again kid," Coach Gottlieb said. "It makes the Broadwood look like a tea party."

Chuck and Red had heard all the stories. How the team all piled into Coach's eight-seat Ford for the road trips. And how some of the other fans were just terrible.

"You should have seen the game in Trenton last week," said Coach. We missed most of our free throws because those crazy fans were tugging on the wires attached to the backboard the whole night. The thing was swaying back and forth like a teeter totter."

"Why do you think the other fans get on you guys so much?" Red asked.

"Well boys, it's a bit of a mixed up world out there I'm afraid. Some people don't much like other people just because of their religion, and some people don't like other people just because of the color of their skin. It doesn't make any sense if you ask me, but it is what it is."

"I figure our job is to let people see that Jewish players can play basketball just as well or better than anybody else, and make our fans proud of us. We're proud of who we are, and not afraid to let people know it. That doesn't make us better than anybody else, but hopefully opens a few people's eyes."

"Tell you what boys.. why don't you join us on the bench tonight. We're playing the Rens and it's worth the price of admission just to see Tarzan play."

"Really, thanks Coach.. we'll be there!" The boys were very excited. They'd never sat on the bench during an actual SPHAS game before, and had heard all the stories about Tarzan Cooper, one of

the league's biggest and best players. He played
for the Harlem Renaissance, but everybody just
called them the Rens.

The Broadwood was packed to the rafters that
night, and what a game it was. The lead went back
and forth, and it was very physical. The biggest
reason was Tarzan.
He stood 6 foot 4
inches tall, and was
one of the toughest
players in the
league.

All night, SPHAS players would run into his picks and end up on the floor. He wasn't a dirty player, just big and strong and tough as nails.

The score was tied in the final seconds, when Harry Litwack took a hard foul driving to the basket. He hit one of the shots, and after the Rens missed a last-second heave, the SPHAS had the win, 61-60.

The team all made a quick exit to the locker room, relieved to get out with a victory. Coach had a few reminders on what they need to work on for next game, but congratulated everyone and said that dinner was on him.

Coach took everyone to a neighborhood Italian restaurant, and as far as the boys were concerned, it was heaven. Food was everywhere, and the guys were in the middle of telling their stories, when it suddenly got very quiet.

Coincidentally, Tarzan and a few members of the Rens had shown up at the same restaurant, but the head waiter wasn't letting them in. "We don't serve coloreds," Red heard him say.

With that, Coach Gottlieb stood up and shouted across the restaurant, "If they don't eat here, we don't eat here," he said powerfully. And with that, all of the members of the team (and the boys) stood up too to show their support. The head waiter looked horrified, and, after a pause, took the Rens to their table.

Tarzan nodded towards the SPHAS table as they went by, and Red realized how much in common the two teams really had. They were both outsiders for different reasons, but connected through the sport of basketball.

"We usually only face prejudice when we're on the court," Cy whispered. "They have to deal with it every day of their lives."

Red knew he was right. And he knew that he'd remember it for as long as he lived.

# MAKING DREAMS COME TRUE

Red was finishing his breakfast the next morning when his Mom sat down next to him.

"So, my son, do you care to tell us where you were last night?" she said.

Red looked at the open newspaper on the table. There was an article about the SPHAS game, and a picture that included someone that looked very familiar... it was Red! He knew he had only one choice. The truth.

"I'm sorry Mom, but I love going to the SPHAS games," Red blurted out. "The team is amazing, and Chuck and I actually get to play in a game for the Outlaws against other kids, and Coach and the players are so nice, and ..."

His mother interrupted. "Now slow down, Louis. I don't know if I like this at all. You know how your father feels about basketball, and I certainly don't like you not telling us the truth."

"I'm really sorry I didn't tell you Mom. It won't happen again. And don't worry. Chuck and I are fine, and Coach Gottlieb and the players really look out for us. Maybe you guys can come to the next game?"

"Well, that will be up to your father," she said. "Why don't you go talk to him about it?"

Red gulped. "Do you think you can tell him?" Red asked, but he knew that was going to be his job.

"You know, Louis, I discussed it with him already, and you might just be surprised by what your father has to say."

Red took a deep breath, and went downstairs to his father's workshop, where he was sanding down some cabinets.

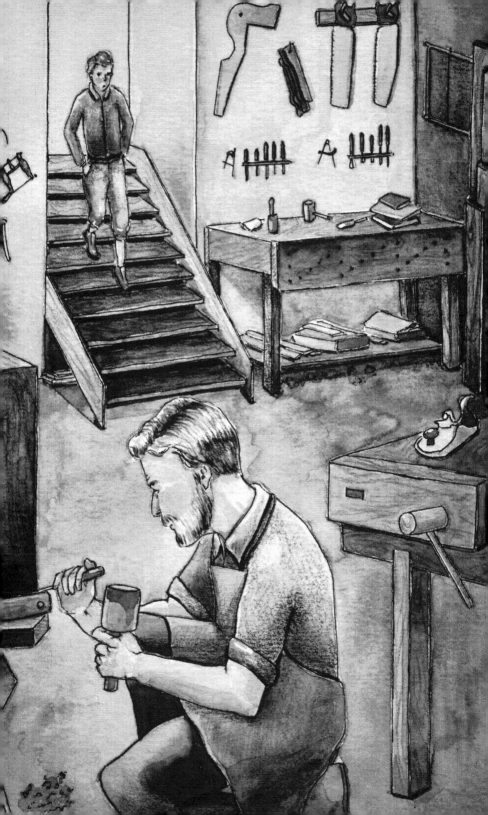

"Sir, I need to apologize," Red started. "On Saturday nights, Chuck and I have been going to the SPHAS basketball games and playing in a kids game and I'm very sorry that I didn't tell you and mom but I didn't think you'd ever let me go."

Red closed his eyes tight and waited to see how bad he was going to get it. What came next, he never expected.

"Louis, Louis, Louis. What is it with you and this basketball?" his father started, but with a softer tone than Red had anticipated. "Always the basketball this and the basketball that. Isn't there more to life?"

"Of course there is Dad, but it's really my favorite thing in the whole world," Red explained. "I love being on a team with the other guys, and I especially love being really good at a sport even though I'm so little."

"You know, Red, when I was your age, my brothers and I were on a soccer team in Russia. We were very good, but our father told us we couldn't play anymore. We needed to work in the shop. I've often thought about playing, and what I would tell my children if they wanted to play a sport."

His father stared at the wall for a long time, soaking in the memory. Red wasn't used to hearing his father talk about his own childhood. He was having a hard time even picturing him as a kid.

Finally, his father finished his thought. "Red, I'll make you a deal," he said. "You start helping me and your brothers in the shop two days a week, and I'll let you play on Saturday nights and with your friends. That's my best offer.. what do you say?"

Red knew it was the best he was going to get, and he took it without hesitation.

"Thank you Sir," he said. "Can I go play today with Chuck?"

"I think not. After lying to your Mother and I about where you've been, you're home for the rest of the weekend. Go get a dustpan and start cleaning up around here.. And if you're not truthful to us again, basketball will be over for you for good."

"Yes sir," said Red. "I understand." Red knew that he got off much better than expected.

"It's good to have dreams," his father said. "Like us coming here to America. But there's a lot of hard work that also has to be done if that dream's going to come true. You need to keep the balance if you're going to succeed."

"I understand Dad," said Red. "I understand." And Red realized that, in fact, he really did.

# ANOTHER CHANCE

A few days later, Red and Chuck got the chance they'd been waiting for. They were back at "The Cage" shooting around, when those two boys showed up, as talkative as ever.

"Did you miss us boys?" one of them called. "We could use another easy win."

Red took a deep breath, and knew what he had to do. "How about a rematch?" he said.

"Is your memory that bad," the boy said. "Don't you remember what we did to you last game. Please don't make us do it again," he said with a laugh.

"I'd love to see you try," Red said. "Let's do this."

Red and Chuck huddled together. "Remember what Cy told us," said Chuck. "Just let your game do your talking, and don't let them get to you. We can take them."

Red knew that this time they were ready. Red and Chuck stuck to their game plan. They took advantage of the other boys' aggressiveness, and actually used it against them. Lots of backdoor cuts, and lots of fakes to get their defender in the air.

Still, it was a close game, with neither side giving an inch. As the game went on, Red noticed that the other boys were talking less and less. Sometimes, they'd even yell at each other.

Red and Chuck were up 14-13, and needed only one more basket to finish it. Red told himself to stay patient, and take what they gave him. Chuck hit him with a pass on the baseline. Red pump-faked to get his defender in the air, the other boy reaching desperately to get a piece of him. Red was too fast though. A cross-over dribble and an easy layup finished the game.

Red and Chuck hugged each other, while the other boys sat on the ground in disbelief. Red remembered how Cy and the SPHAS acted after a win.

"Good game," Red said, putting out his hand. The boy looked at him, first with anger, but then with a bit of a smile. "Good game," the boy said, shaking Red's hand. "You guys must have been practicing."

"Yeah, a little," Red said with a smile, thinking about all he'd learned on and off the court since their first meeting. "You guys are good though."

"Thanks," the boy said. "My name's Lucas."

"I'm Red and this is Chuck," Red said. "We play with the SPHAS."

# FOR CHUCK

Louis had sat in silence, listening to his Grandpa's story as the ice cream melted in front of him.

"Grandpa, did you and Chuck ever get to play for the SPHAS?" Louis asked, breathless. "Did you ever win a championship?"

"Only one of us did, Louis," he said. "We went to college at Villanova together for two years, but when World War II came, I was sent to the Air Force and Chuck became a Lieutenant in the Marine Corps. He was sent to a place called Iwo Jima, and died a hero fighting for our country."

Neither of them said anything for a few seconds. "When I came back to Philadelphia, I played for the SPHAS, and we won the championship. I dedicated the season to Chuck, and gave the trophy to his parents. And when your grandma and I had our first son, we named him Chuck... your father."

"Wow, I didn't know that Dad was named after him. I'm sorry Grandpa. He was your best friend, wasn't he?" Louis asked.

"He sure was Louis. He sure was. And I've thought about him every day since. It's one of the reasons I started coaching and traveling with the Globetrotters. I wanted to teach the game of basketball and all the lessons that Chuck and I learned to as many people as I could."

"I know that Chuck would be proud of you, Grandpa. And your mom and dad too."

"I think you're right, Louis," Red said. "I think you're right. Now, let's get you home."

# EPILOGUE

After a playing career that would include an NBA championship with the Baltimore Bullets in 1948, Red Klotz went on to become founder and owner of the Washington Generals, the regular opponents to the Harlem Globetrotters.

Red coached and played for the team for many years, playing (and losing) more than 10,000 games against the Globetrotters in front of millions of fans worldwide. In 1971, he helped to engineer the Generals' last win over the Globetrotters, snapping a 2,400-game win streak in the process.

One of the greatest ambassadors the sport has ever known, Red introduced the game of basketball (and lessons of sportsmanship and tolerance) to popes, presidents, kings, and children of all ages

Red has yet to be inducted into the Naismith Memorial Basketball Hall of Fame, despite the efforts of many friends, colleagues and sportswriters. He is now 91 and lives with his wife Gloria in Margate City, NJ. He has six children and 16 grandchildren. Red played basketball regularly into his late 80s, and his shooting prowess remains legendary.

Eddie Gottlieb would go on to be one of the founders of the NBA, and owner of the Philadelphia Warriors NBA franchise. For more than 25 years, he was also the official schedule maker for the NBA, and is responsible for many of the league's rules. He was inducted into the Hall of Fame in 1971.

Charles T. "Tarzan" Cooper was a member of many great Renaissance squads, including the one that won the 1939 World Professional Basketball Tournament in which Cooper was named tournament MVP. He was enshrined into the Hall of Fame in 1977.

The PA Announcer at the SPHAS home games, Dave Zinkoff, would go on to be the legendary PA voice of the Philadelphia Warriors and Sixers, and still has a banner hanging in the Sixers' arena today.

The SPHAS franchise existed from 1917-1948, winning multiple championships in the Eastern League and American Basketball League, including seven titles in 13 years from 1933-1946. The team was inducted into the International Jewish Sports Hall of Fame in Israel in 1996, and their legend continues to grow among basketball fans everywhere.

# AFTERWORD

*Red Klotz: In His Own Words*

I grew up in the depression.

As a kid, though, we didn't understand the
depression. As kids growing up in south
Philadelphia, there wasn't such a thing as being
. poor. Nobody was starving. If we had a pair of
converse sneakers, a stick, and a baseball, we
enjoyed ourselves. We played games out in the
street. We played baseball together. We played
basketball together. We'd go to dances together.
Soon you learned to realize we're all the same. We
had different religions and so on, but all we wanted
was respect. And that's what my mother and father
taught us: respect your neighbors.

My father was a carpenter and a cabinet-maker until he had an accident in his eye, but he made a living, fortunately. During the bad years, he had a job with Fels Naptha Soap Company, which still exists. I remember we used to make beer for my father in the cellar. One time we put too much yeast in the beer and it got hot and you could hear this BOOM from the kitchen.

To make money as a kid, I'd go to the Philadelphia Eagles games at Shibe Park. I was about ten or eleven years old and I would try to sell peanuts or something in the stands. At that time, the players didn't even have to wear helmets. You can find photos of guys tackling each other and some guys have leather helmets on and some guys didn't.

My dad and my mother didn't know I was playing sports as well. I used to dump my bag out the back window and get on the trolley car to go to 5th and Bainbridge to play. It was a cage—literally a cage – that just gave you a little bit more room than the top of the ceiling to shoot the ball. So you have to be dead accurate or you hit the ceiling. Chuck and I would beat everybody we played.

*"Red" Klotz at 2 years-old holding ball.*

I met my best friend Chuck Drizen when playing for the Outlaws. He was a beautiful person. When I met him, he was playing for Germantown and I was playing for Southern, but we also played for the Outlaws. He was my best friend.  There was a guy that you loved as a person. You had to love this guy. This guy would do anything to help, whatever. Everybody considered him a good friend.

Later, when the World War II started, Chuck and I actually wanted to get in the Marines together. I was near-sighted. Even though I could shoot the heck out of a ball, I was near-sighted so the Marines wouldn't take me. Still I ended up going into the service before he did. He was worried about me, but he ended up in Iwo Jima. I was hoping he wouldn't end up there. See Chuck penetrated too deep into the island. It was unbelievable what they did with what little they had. The Japanese had that place targeted off every foot. It was just a massacre. We lost Chuck. We lost a lot good people. I named my son after him.

I had started playing for the Outlaws when I was 10 or 11 years old. We played the preliminary match before the great South Philadelphia Hebrew Association teams (the SPHAS), who had some of the best players in the country. If you came to a SPHAS game, you sat up in the balcony of the Broadwood Hotel ballroom, watching the game on the floor below. Everybody was dressed. You came to see the great team but you also knew there was going be a dance after the game. The team had their own little band, with Gil Fitch, which played after the game and for a great deal of the fans, that's where they met their wives. It was a beautiful affair.

For a long time, the SPHAS were an all-Jewish team. Some say, "That's unusual, that's odd." But it wasn't really because you had Irish teams, you had Jewish teams, you had Italian teams, all depending on where you lived, the area you lived in. We just were not welcome in other areas. I mean, if you pass through that area, you better be moving fast or you can be in trouble. You wouldn't have a Jewish guy playing on an Italian team when he couldn't even get a walk into the neighborhood. It wasn't like we were scared or nothing, it's just the way it was back then.

The SPHAS were proud of who they were, though. There was nothing to be ashamed of. It was just that they had a lot of competition—people trying

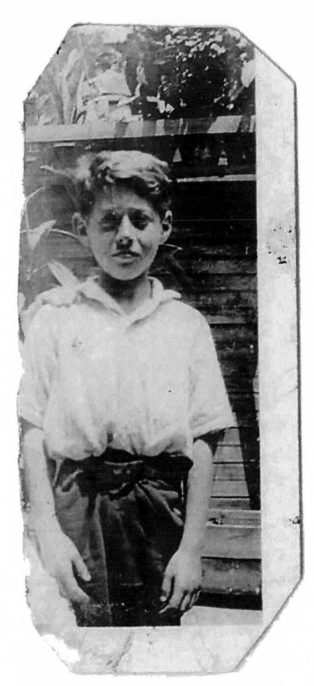

*"Red" Klotz at 8 years old.*

to prove that they were nobody. It turned out that the SPHAS were not only not nobody, but that they were better than almost everybody. Still the SPHAS went through some odd experiences for that reason early on, when players like Harry Litwack were on the team. Most of it was racial. You know, it was the threats from the audience: cat calls and all that stuff. They had people trying to poke a player with a needle or throw something down at them.

The best way to handle it was by beating them to teach them respect. And generally the players who we played against, eventually not only gave respect, but became friends. These players loved basketball and they figured if we love basketball, then we both love something together. We both loved the same game. I guess we figured out "they're okay." It had nothing to do with religion after that point, it had to do with talent. Gradually it all worked out beautifully.

First thing to make sure you are a good ball player is to love of the game. That love demands you learn the fundamentals. When you learn the fundamentals it means you respect the four other guys on the court with you. If they know you are looking for them, if they cut and you give them a good pass, then they make an easy basket because of that pass, they will think, "Hey, this guy really is a team player." You make them want to look for you as well.

Today, we are not teaching the kids that kind of sportsmanship. Today they are teaching kids to break the other player's nose. You don't try to cripple a player to try to win the game. This happens all the time. You knock one of the super key players out, you're going to win that game, unless you got a great bench. In the NBA playoffs, if you watch, they're trying to knock out one of the superstars, so they can win the championship. They shouldn't be doing that. Sportsmanship has to come back. Being a team player has to come back.

You had to be a team player in those days, even as a kid. And because of that, when I was on the Outlaws, we never lost a game. Then I moved into the SPHAS reserve and we beat everybody—I never lost a game. I was actually with the last SPHA's team that won the championship in the American League in 1942 with Eddie Gottlieb, who was my first pro coach. I not only played with a championship team, but I got to be the coach, the manager, and the driver. Eddie Gottlieb took the SPHAS with him when he passed away.

*"Red" Klotz, Back Row, End Left.*
*1st Team, "Outlaws".*

I created the Washington Generals to compete with the Harlem Globetrotters in 1952. Now my first game with the SPHAS, we played the Globetrotters in an exhibition game before the season started and we beat them. In fact, every time I came across them, as player or coach, we almost beat them or it was like an extra period, a point difference. So they had a belly-full of me. When the Globetrotters beat the Lakers, the Minneapolis Lakers, not one time, but twice, the team became famous immediately. They were not supposed to beat Minneapolis, but they beat them. Sure enough Abe Saperstein, who was building the Globetrotters, called me in the office and said to me, "Look Red, we're now going to be moving into big buildings. I'm going to need tough opposition steadily for the tours. I'd like you to get a team together." This was the Washington Generals.

Still, the misunderstanding to this very day is that "Hey they got huge, so they made sure they never lose again." That's not true at all. There's my proof right there. We don't let them win. Even in practice, we almost beat them. It don't matter what you got against you, it's more the reason that you have to prove that you can do what your talents demand. And when you walk off that court, believe me, that audience will have changed their opinion about that Washington Generals team that loses all the time. I said, "Don't worry about that final score. It's not in your power to do anything except to say, 'Hey, you know me don't you?'" "Yes, I sure do, you're one heck of a ball player, I could really see you in a league or something." So when asked about losing to the Globetrotters so much, I kid about it. I say, "As a kid I never lost a game and as an old man I lost 4,000 games."

When I was a little kid, I would have dreams of things I wanted to be when I grow up. I wanted to see the world. I wanted to see Rome. I wanted to see things I heard on the radio. It probably should never have happened, but it did. I saw the world many times over with the Generals and Globetrotters. I saw big cities and small cities and all these different countries. But it would never have happened if I didn't play basketball.

All my dreams that I had as a kid came true because of basketball.

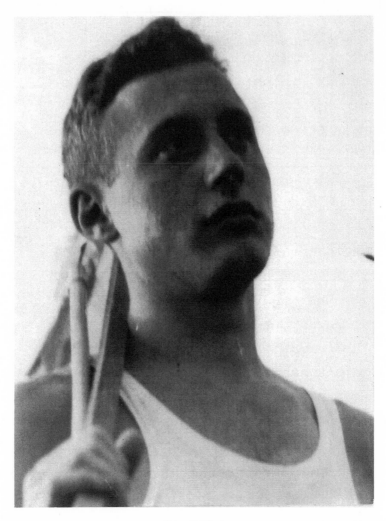

*"Red" Klotz*